1

1. Introduction

In this paper we investigate whether oil price changes can predict short-term stock returns in oil-exporting countries, and we link the strength of the predictive relation to institutional quality, for which we use Transparency International's Corruption Perceptions Index (henceforth, CPI) as a proxy. We find that returns are predictable in half the countries we consider, and that predictability is stronger for countries with weaker institutions. Based on the extant literature, we posit that institutional quality is negatively related to the propensity to consume oil windfalls, directly through pro-cyclical fiscal policies or indirectly through inefficient expenditure, and that return predictability reflects the extent to which oil windfalls are consumed locally rather than, for instance, invested through a sovereign wealth fund.[1]

Our work bridges two separate literature strands, one on return predictability and one on the interaction of fiscal policy and institutional quality. It is also related to the literature on the predictability of the business cycle using oil prices, and to studies of the "resource curse," which focus on how the economic development of resource-rich countries interacts with weak institutions.

The literature on whether oil prices can predict stock returns is largely focused on developed markets. Huang, Masulis, and Stoll (1996) study the lead-lag relation between U.S. stock returns and returns on oil futures. With the exception of oil companies, they find weak correlations. In an analysis of how oil prices interact with changes in expected returns and cash flows, Jones and Kaul (1996) show that lagged quarterly changes in oil prices can, in isolation, predict quarterly stock-market returns for the United States, Canada, and Japan. Driesprong, Jacobsen, and Maat (2008) conduct an extensive predictability study and find that oil prices have weak predictive power

---

[1] Pieschacon (2012) theoretically demonstrates that policies that insulate the economy from oil fluctuations seem to be welfare improving compared with pro-cyclical fiscal policies.

in the case of developing economies. Kilian and Park (2009) highlight that the implications of oil prices shocks for U.S. stock returns depend on whether prices have changed in response to supply or demand shocks, with the latter explaining a larger fraction of stock returns. In this paper, we follow Jones and Kaul (1996) and Driesprong, Jacobsen, and Maat (2008), and remain agnostic as to whether the predictability is driven by demand or supply shocks.

Persson (2002) highlights that political institutions influence economic choices, including "fiscal policy, broadly defined to include rents sought by corrupt politicians" (page 884). Fatás and Mihov (2003) show that countries that deploy more prudent fiscal policies face lower output volatility and higher economic growth, and that such countries are characterized by majoritarian and constrained political systems. Alesina, Tabellini, and Campante (2008) find evidence that corrupt democracies have more pro-cyclical fiscal policies. Pieschacon (2012) analyzes the role of fiscal policy on how oil shocks affect consumption and relative prices in oil-exporting small open economies through a dynamic stochastic general equilibrium (DSGE) model. Countries like Norway, which invests oil windfalls internationally, see smaller fluctuations in domestic variables like output or the price of non-tradeable goods in response to an increase in oil revenues than countries like Mexico, whose fiscal policies allow consumption and other domestic variables to fluctuate more closely with oil revenues.

Studies of return predictability focus on the short term, but oil prices also have implications at the business-cycle frequency if one considers macroeconomic variables such as output or unemployment. Hamilton (1983, 1996) highlights that shocks to oil prices often precede recessions in the United States. Barsky and Kilian (2004) emphasize that oil prices are endogenous with respect to economic conditions in the United States, and that, while oil shocks likely contribute to macroeconomic fluctuations, their role is not necessarily pivotal. Ravazzolo and Rothman (2013) find that U.S. GDP growth can be predicted, out-of-sample, with real time refiner's acquisition cost of crude oil. See Hamilton (2011) and Kilian (2008) for recent literature overviews.

The long-run effect of oil income on the economic growth of oil-producing countries depends on a number of factors, chiefly the level and persistence of oil revenues (Esfahani, Mohaddes, and Pesaran, 2014). However, the institutional characteristics of a country also play a role, since they influence how efficiently these revenues are spent. Sachs and Werner (1995) find that the abundance of natural resources is negatively related to economic growth. Mehlum, Moene, and Torvik (2006) document that this "resource curse" is only found in countries characterized by inefficient institutions. Mauro (1995) also highlights that corruption and bureaucratic inefficiency significantly reduce both investment and economic growth. Leite and Weidmann (1999) and Vicente (2010) suggest that the causality can run in either direction, and that the availability of natural resources can reduce the efficiency of a country's institutions. James (2015) interprets the resource curse in terms of commodity price trends, since resource-rich countries grow more slowly when the commodity they depend on experiences price declines. See van der Ploeg (2011) for an encompassing review of the literature on this topic.

Analyzing the interaction between economic growth and institutional quality is typically complicated by endogeneity issues, and several authors have focused on narrower questions to obtain a cleaner picture of how economic behavior is affected by institutional quality, broadly defined to include cultural norms. For instance, Ichino and Maggi (2000) study confidential personnel data from an Italian bank and find that cultural differences explain effort/rent extraction. Fisman and Miguel (2007) highlight how cultural norms foster corruption by studying the relation between a country's measured corruption and how often the country's United Nations diplomats left traffic tickets unpaid in New York City, where traffic violations committed by diplomats were not sanctioned before 2002. Ebeke, Omgba, and Laajaj (2015) find that university students choose to specialize in rent-seeking fields more often when institutions are weak.

While the literature on the impact of corruption/institutional quality on economic growth generally acknowledges the endogeneity of the two variables of interest (e.g., Mauro, 1995), our analysis assumes that the institutional quality impacts fiscal policy, and not vice versa. The reason is that fiscal policy is a variable over which policymakers have direct control, which reduces reverse-causality concerns. Our empirical strategy is broadly comparable to Alesina, Tabellini, and Campante (2008), who study the pro-cyclicality of fiscal policy conditional on corruption, and use panel regressions in which corruption is not instrumented.

The rest of the paper is organized as follows: Section 2 describes the data and the empirical implementation; Section 3 presents the results; and Section 4 concludes.

2. Data and empirical implementation

2.1 Data

Our sample includes countries for which oil exports are a significant source of revenue, measured with the value of oil exports over gross domestic product (GDP). The value of oil exports is calculated by multiplying the average yearly price for a barrel of West Texas Intermediate oil (WTI, from the Federal Reserve Economic Data website) by the number of oil barrels exported in a given year (crude oil including lease condensate, from the website of the U.S. Energy Information Administration). GDP in current U.S. dollars (USD) is from the World Bank (series NY.GDP.MKTP.CD).

Table 1 shows the countries for which (1) the oil revenue/GDP ratio is above 1% in 1995, 2003, and 2010, and (2) data on the market capitalization of listed companies to GDP (series CM.MKT.LCAP.GD.ZS from the World Bank) is available in the same years. Requiring that the ratio is above 1% in each of the three years ensures that oil revenues are a meaningful fraction of GDP throughout the sample. We consider the three years above because, as detailed later in this Section, the return series are mostly available from the mid-1990s. Finally, we only consider countries for which data on stock market capitalization to GDP is available to ensure that we can evaluate whether our results are driven by heterogeneity in financial development. As shown in Section 3, this is not the case.

Due to constraints on the availability of returns data, we exclude two of the countries in our sample (Iran and Trinidad and Tobago). Hence, we study 15 oil exporting countries that cover the Middle East, Africa, the Americas, Asia, and Europe. The importance of oil exports relative to GDP varies significantly in the cross-section, ranging from 40% to the low single digits. Over time, the ratio is generally stable, dropping sharply only for Nigeria. There is significant heterogeneity in financial development, with Canada, Kuwait, and Malaysia having stock market capitalization in excess of GDP, and Ecuador, Nigeria, and Venezuela having relatively small stock markets.

Our proxy for institutional quality is the Corruption Perceptions Index (CPI) maintained by Transparency International. The index ranks countries on the basis of the perceived corruption of their public sectors, and it consolidates data from various independent institutions that analyze governance and business climate. CPI data for all of the countries in our sample is available starting in 2003, and we measure the institutional quality of each country with the average CPI between 2003 and 2013. We should note that, while interpreting corruption measures as proxies for "institutional quality" is to some extent arbitrary, previous studies have already highlighted this connection in light of conceptual overlaps and the empirical challenges in distinguishing the two.[2]

---

[2]   Mehlum, Moene, and Torvik (2006, pg.3) note that institutions conducive to rent-seeking behavior are characterized by, among other items, "weak rule of law, malfunctioning bureaucracy, and corruption". Conversely, the survey-based measure of corruption built by Vicente (2010) probes the quality of a wide range of public services, including courts of law and the bureaucracy, and Mauro (1995) suggests that evaluating the efficiency of the judiciary and bureaucratic systems can improve the measurement of corruption. Several measures of corruption are available. Mauro (1995) studies Business International indexes, while Alesina, Tabellini, and Campante (2008) and Fisman and Miguel (2007) use the corruption measure of Kaufmann, Kraay, and Mastruzzi (2005, 2006). Fisman and Miguel (2007) find that this measure is highly correlated with the rankings of Transparency International that we use in this paper.

We report the average CPI in the first column of Table 2. The index ranges between 0 and 100, with the latter indicating the lowest possible level of perceived corruption. There are large differences across countries, with Canada and Norway scoring highly, and Nigeria and Russia at the other end of the spectrum. Interestingly, a comparison of Tables 1 and 2 shows that higher perceived corruption is not necessarily associated with higher dependence on oil exports. For instance, Oman is highly dependent on oil and has the third highest CPI score in the sample. In Table 3 we show that the corruption index is generally stable over time, which implies that we can use the average CPI as a proxy for institutional quality throughout the sample, following the approach of Alesina, Tabellini, and Campante (2008).

We obtain stock returns from Thomson Reuters' Datastream. Following Driesprong, Jacobsen, and Maat (2008), we use MSCI indexes when available (see Table 2 for details and summary statistics). While our analysis is based on total return indexes, in which dividends are reinvested, excluding dividends has little effect on the results. All indexes are expressed in USD, and data is available through December 2013. Some of the series go back to at least the 1980s, however a fair number of them start in the mid-to-late 1990s. We ensure that the regression results are comparable across countries by only considering data from January 1995 if the series are available from an earlier date. Table 2 shows the starting dates for the various return series.

2.2 Empirical Implementation

Our research design draws from the results in Driesprong, Jacobsen, and Maat (2008), who conduct an extensive predictability study, and find that oil price changes can predict local stock returns for a large cross-section of countries. They conclude that the predictability is not due to a potential co-movement of oil prices with risk premia, but to delays in incorporating oil-related information into stock prices.

The key assumption of this paper is that, because of the delayed response identified by Driesprong, Jacobsen, and Maat (2008), stock returns in t will respond to oil price changes in $t-1$. In addition, we posit that the strength of the predictive regression will vary on the basis of institutional quality, since lower institutional quality implies that a country is more likely to consume oil windfalls rather than smooth their business-cycle effects by, for instance, investing the proceeds through a sovereign wealth fund. Our assumption that institutional quality affects fiscal policy is based on the results in Alesina, Tabellini, and Campante (2008), who find that corrupt democracies have more pro-cyclical fiscal policies, and in Fatás and Mihov (2003), who show that constrained political systems lead to less volatile fiscal policies.

The main advantage of our approach is that we do not need to model cyclically-adjusted fiscal policy, which, as noted by Fatás and Mihov (2003), is complicated by the simultaneity of output and fiscal policy. Instead, we use equity returns' reaction to oil price changes as a proxy for expectations of fiscal policy. While our methodology is simple to implement, we need to rule out alternative explanations for the relation between institutions and predictability, which we do in the next Section.

Figure 1 shows a clearly positive relation between institutional quality and the size of each country's sovereign wealth fund.[3] The regression slope reported in the Figure, which we can interpret as the elasticity of sovereign wealth funds' size relative to institutional quality, is equal to 3.96. While the low number of observations makes statistical inference problematic, the positive relation shown in the Figure supports our assumption that higher institutional quality is associated with higher smoothing of oil prices's impact on the business cycle.

---

[3]   Data on sovereign wealth funds' assets is from the Sovereign Wealth Fund Institute, as of January 2015. Figure 1 does not show four of the fifteen countries we study, because data on sovereign funds' assets are unavailable. These countries are Colombia, Ecuador, Egypt, and Tunisia.

We emphasize that Figure 1 is based on data that are qualitatively different from those we use when studying return predictability. In particular, sovereign wealth funds invest in foreign assets (Kotter and Lel, 2011), while we focus on local equity market returns. Additionally, sovereign wealth funds' assets are stock data, while equity market returns reflect investment flows in and out of stock markets. Finally, sovereign wealth funds' assets reflect past government decisions, while investment flows into the stock market reflect expectations of future economic conditions, including anticipated fiscal policies. Given that institutional characteristics are persistent, as shown in Table 3, they can explain the way the CPI variable is related to both return predictability and sovereign wealth funds' assets.

We need to clarify why we study the effect of oil price changes on future returns rather than contemporaneous returns. The reason is that oil price changes are correlated with stock market volatility, especially when the price of oil drops.[4] As a result, the effect of oil price changes on contemporaneous returns can be obfuscated by simultaneous changes in expected returns driven by fluctuation in aggregate risk, as reflected in higher volatility. Our research design allows us to obtain a cleaner estimate of the impact of oil price changes on stock prices, since aggregate equity market indexes incorporate general news about the state of the economy more quickly than they incorporate sectoral news about oil prices (see Driesprong, Jacobsen, and Maat, 2008 and Hong, Torous, and Valkanov, 2007 for a thorough discussion). As a result, the predictive relation reflects sectoral economic news (including oil price changes) rather than changes in risk premia.

The bulk of our results are based on the following predictive regression:

$$r_t^i = \alpha + \beta_0 r_t^{S\&P} + \beta_1 oil_{t-1} + \epsilon_t^i, \tag{1}$$

---

[4]   Over the 1995-2013 period that we study, the correlation between monthly oil price changes and monthly S&P 500 return volatility is -28% (-40% if we only consider negative returns). Excluding October 2008, when both oil prices and stock prices had outsized changes, the correlations are -15% and -28%, respectively.

where r_t^i is the log return on country i's stock market index in month t and in excess of the riskless rate, $r_t^{S\&P}$ is the excess log return on the S&P 500 index in month t, and oil_{t-1} is the log change in oil prices in month $t-1$.[5] Unless specified otherwise, local stock returns include dividend reinvestment, and oil price changes are calculated using WTI prices. The riskless rate is the appropriately compounded 3-month Treasury Bill rate (series DTB3 from the Federal Reserve Economic Date website). The coefficients are estimated with ordinary least squares, and statistical significance is evaluated using heteroskedasticity-consistent standard errors.

The regressions include the contemporaneous return on the S&P 500 index to account for broad market movements, so to minimize the risk that oil price changes reflect economic news about the U.S., which is the largest oil consumer during our sampling period. In some of the robustness checks, we include the S&P 500 log dividend-price ratio as a predictor to understand whether oil price changes are proxies for valuation ratios (both S&P 500 returns and the dividend-price ratio are from the dataset used by Goyal and Welch, 2008, and available on Amit Goyal's website).[6] The log dividend-price ratio is highly autocorrelated, which can bias predictive regression coefficients (Stambaugh, 1999). As a consequence, we use the procedure in Amihud, Hurvich, and Wang (2009) to obtain both the coefficients and the standard errors.

Our analysis is based on a set of country-specific regressions. We do not use a panel regression setup for the following reasons. First, our primary interest is to evaluate the response of equity market returns to oil price changes separately for each country. Second, we let the slope coefficients of contemporaneous S&P 500 returns vary across countries to account for varying degrees of correlation between the local and U.S. stock markets. Using a plain vanilla panel estimator would

---

[5] We include returns on the S&P 500 index rather than returns on global equity indexes (such as the MSCI ACWI) since, as noted by Kilian and Park (2009), real crude oil prices are largely subject to the same shocks that impact the U.S. economy, and, by extension, the U.S. stock market.

[6] See, among many other studies, Campbell and Shiller (1988), Fama and French (1988), Campbell and Thompson (2008), and Goyal and Welch (2008).

average both the oil and S&P 500 coefficients across countries, and introducing dummy variables to differentiate country effects on both the oil and S&P 500 slope parameters is tantamount to running a set of country-specific regressions.

In our first set of regressions, we lag the oil price series by one day before calculating monthly oil price changes. As a result, the change in month t is computed from the second-to-last day in month $t-1$ to the second-to-last day in month t. The reason is that we compare predictability in markets across a wide range of time zones, from Malaysia to Canada. Without lagging the oil time series, oil price news on a given day could be reflected in Canadian stock prices on the same day, and in Malaysian stock prices the following day. As a consequence, cross-country differences in predictability could be due to asynchronous trading. In some results we also lag the oil time series by two or three days before calculating oil price changes; in these cases we are using lags to evaluate how long it takes for information in oil prices to be reflected in stock prices, in line with the analysis in Driesprong, Jacobsen, and Maat (2008). We use a superscript to indicate by how many days the oil series is lagged: oil^a (one day), oil^b (two days), and oil^c (three days).

3. Results

As shown in Table 4, we find statistically significant predictability for seven of the 15 countries we study. The first three columns of each panel show slopes and t-stats for regressions in which only lagged oil price changes are included as predictors. The predictive strength, statistical significance, and fit generally decline as the number of days by which the oil series are lagged increases, although for all the seven countries the predictive slopes are still statistically significant at 10% when lagging the oil series by three days (note that in all cases we regress one-month ahead equity returns on monthly oil price changes; the daily lags indicate how many days we skip between the oil price change in month $t-1$ and the equity return in month t). With the exception of Kuwait and Oman, the adjusted R^2s are fairly small, which is typical for predictive regressions and is due to the volatility of returns. The patterns are largely unchanged when including contemporaneous S&P 500 excess returns in the regressions, with the oil slopes (β_1 in Eq. 1) slightly smaller, and the statistical significance higher. These results support the hypothesis that oil prices reflect, in part, information about the state of the U.S. economy.

Our findings are noticeably different from those of Driesprong, Jacobsen, and Maat (2008, Table 5), who provide evidence of no predictability for the seven countries that, in our analysis, have predictable returns. The discrepancy is driven by samples that overlap only partially. We find no predictability when we run the predictability regressions with samples ending in April 2003, which is when the sample of Driesprong, Jacobsen, and Maat (2008) ends.

Driesprong, Jacobsen, and Maat (2008) conclude that the predictive power of oil is not driven by risk premia, but by delays in information processing. We find evidence that predictability is driven by a similar mechanism in our data as well. In Table 5 we report predictive slopes and t-stats from regressions of returns on three lags of oil price changes for the seven countries that have significant slopes in Table 4. We expect to find no longer-term predictive power if predictability is driven by slow information diffusion rather than changes in risk premia associated with oil price fluctuations. For five countries, only the first lag of oil price changes has predictive power. In the case of Kuwait, the second lag has a statistically significant slope, while for Oman it is the third lag that is weakly statistically significant. Overall, these results suggest that predictability is due to frictions in the diffusion of oil price information rather than changes in risk premia, as documented by Driesprong, Jacobsen, and Maat (2008).

We now turn to how the quality of a country's institutions affects the predictive regression, and we should point out that our analysis going forward is largely based on a visual representation of the results. The reason is that our sample selection criteria – discussed in Section 2.1 – limit the sample to 15 countries, which constrains our ability to carry out a formal statistical analysis in the cross-section.

In Figure 2 we show scatter plots of the slopes of predictive regressions (vertical axis) against the log CPI, with red markers indicating countries for which the predictive relation is statistically significant (the absolute value of the t-stat being greater than 1.65). We use the log of the index because Canada and Norway have a much higher score than the other countries, and they would exert a strong leverage effect if the index were not transformed. In the top left chart, the slopes are computed from regressions that lag the oil price series by one day and that do not include the contemporaneous return on the S&P 500. In the remaining regressions, the contemporaneous return on the S&P 500 is included, and the oil price series is lagged by one, two, and three days, as indicated. All charts show that there is no relation between predictive slopes and institution quality without conditioning on statistical significance. When considering statistically significant slopes only, however, lower institutional quality is associated with stronger predictability.

We argue that the absence of predictability in some of the countries shown in Table 4 and also in Figure 2 is likely to be driven by the low liquidity of the respective equity markets. Pastor and Stambaugh (2003) study the asset-pricing implications of liquidity, which they define as "the ability to trade large quantities [of assets] quickly, at low cost, and without moving the price". In countries with less developed financial markets, one may observe relatively large price movements that reflect a lack of liquidity rather than changes in fundamentals. As a consequence, it may be more difficult to establish a relation between stock returns and lagged oil prices.

The rightmost columns of Table 1 show the ratios of market capitalization of listed companies to GDP (which we take as a measure of financial development) in 1995, 2003, and 2010. Using 2003 data to proxy for the level throughout the sample period, the seven countries for which we find statistically significant predictability have an average ratio of 58%, compared to 36% for countries with statistically insignificant predictive slopes. The median ratios, which reduce the impact of Malaysia's outsized value, are 54% and 16%, respectively, indicating that countries for which we find no predictability have substantially less developed financial markets. We should emphasize that, as discussed below, the pattern of predictive power across financial development does not match the pattern of predictive power across institutional quality very well. Overall, these results suggest a threshold effect of financial development: identifying predictability is difficult for low levels of financial development, but higher levels are not associated with the strength of the predictive relation.

In Figure 3 we evaluate whether the relation between predictability and institutional quality can be explained by leverage, financial development, or the importance of oil exports relative to the economy.[7] To save space, we only show results when the oil price series is lagged by two days. The top left chart, which is taken from Figure 2 to facilitate the comparison with the remaining charts, shows CPI values against predictive slopes calculated when including contemporaneous S&P 500 returns.[8] The first alternative explanation we consider is leverage: if companies in countries with low institutional quality have higher leverage, their stock prices would mechanically be more reactive to changes in oil prices, and the predictive slopes would be larger. In the top right chart of Figure 3, we plot the slopes against the log-ratio of private-sector domestic credit to GDP. We can

---

[7] Our measure for leverage is private-sector domestic credit to GDP (series FS.AST.PRVT.GD.ZS from the World Bank). The values shown are averages between 2003 and 2013, to cover a period similar to the one for which CPI is available. Financial development and oil exports are defined in Section 2.1.

[8] In the Figures, we show average values for the various country-specific variables. The CPI data is only available from 2003 for all the countries we study, and, for comparability reasons, averages for the other variables are also calculated starting from 2003 to 2012, the year through which when most variables are available. In the case of private-sector domestic credit to GDP, data is only available through 2006. Stock market capitalization data is unavailable in 2007 and 2008 for Venezuela.

14

see that higher predictive power is actually associated with lower leverage, the opposite of what we would expect if the predictabiliy/institutional quality pattern was due to leverage. The fact that the two top charts look very similar is consistent with the observation that legal investor protection is positively related with the development of financial markets, including debt markets (La Porta, Lopez-De-Silanes, Shleifer, and Vishny, 1997).

The bottom left chart of Figure 3 shows the predictive slopes against the capitalization of listed companies relative to GDP, which we consider a measure of financial development. Russia, which is the country with the largest predictive slope, has a fairly developed stock market. Tunisia, on the other hand, ranks lowest in financial development even though predictability is about as strong as for Canada, which has the largest stock market relative to GDP. The predictive slope for Oman is about the same as in the case of Kuwait and Saudi Arabia, even though Oman's stock market is relatively small.

The last chart in Figure 3 evaluates the effect of oil-export dependence on the predictive relation. It could be the case, for instance, that a larger predictive slope simply reflects that a country derives a larger amount of revenue from exporting oil. The bottom right chart shows that the Middle-Eastern countries export significantly more oil than the rest in relation to GDP, but predictability is not commensurately stronger for these countries relative to Russia or Indonesia. Indonesia derives the smallest amount of revenue from oil exports, yet it has the second strongest predictability below Russia and just above Kuwait.

We provide an additional set of robustness checks in Figure 4. First, we exclude the October 2008 oil price change from the sample (top left). Second, we use Brent oil prices instead of WTI prices (top right). Third, we consider returns without dividend reinvestment (bottom left). Finally, we include the lagged S&P 500 price dividend ratio as a regressor in place of the contemporaneous

S&P 500 return. Oil prices experienced their largest negative return in October 2008, and we exclude that month's observation to evaluate whether it exerts an undue leverage on the results. The predictive relation becomes statistically insignificant for Saudi Arabia, but it remains broadly unchanged for the other countries. We should highlight that, while we need to be aware of the potential effect of large oil price movements on statistical inference, these movements generate substantial variation in the countries' available revenue and thus provide identification.

Predictability is weaker when using Brent prices (from the Federal Reserve Economic Data) instead of WTI prices, with the slopes becoming statistically insignificant for Indonesia and Saudi Arabia, and the relation between CPI and the slopes being less steep overall. While price changes for Brent and WTI oil are highly correlated, the correlation varies over time. It is equal to 89% between 1995 and 2013, but it is higher early in the sample and it peaks at 96% between 2002 and 2004. It is lower in the second half of the sample, with a minimum of 70% between 2011 and 2013. As noted above in this Section, statistical significance is driven by data in the second half of the sample. This observation, together with the fact that the correlation is lower in the second half of the sample, suggests that differences in the results when using Brent prices are due to weaker correlation in the years that provide economic identification.

As shown in the bottom panels of Figure 4, excluding dividends from the calculation of returns and including the lagged log dividend-price ratio does not alter our predictability results.

3.1 Institutions, oil prices, and equity values

The results discussed above can be used to approximate the magnitude of the impact of institutional quality on how oil revenue is spent. We do so by taking the difference between predictive slopes for countries with high and low institutional quality. The top left chart of Figure 3, which we take as representative of the results, shows that the difference between the interpolated statistically significant slopes at the highest and lowest CPI levels is slightly greater than 0.1. If we round this difference down to 0.1, a 1% increase in oil prices translates into 0.1% higher stock market returns for countries with low institutional quality relative to those with high institutional quality.

Note that the slope coefficients are informative about the impact of oil price changes on equity prices, not on asset prices. The reason is that equity-holders have a claim on the firm's assets which is subordinated to that of debt-holders. In order to calculate the effect of oil price changes on the value of the assets held by listed companies we need information on the liabilities issued by the firms included in the stock market indexes, which is unavailable for most countries. We can, however, use a formula that describes the relation between the slope coefficients of equity and asset returns to estimate the effect of oil price changes on asset values, for different leverage levels.[9] For a ratio of debt to equity equal to 1 (or 3), a 1% increase in oil prices would result in asset values 0.050% (or 0.025%) higher in countries with low institutional quality relative to those with high institutional quality.

The pattern of access to debt markets across countries, as shown in Figure 3, makes our results conservative. The reason is that based on this Figure, countries with weaker institutions have lower leverage and – as discussed above – the sensitivity of stock returns to oil price changes depends on the leverage of the companies in the stock index: the higher the leverage, the higher the sensitivity. If their leverage were increased to match that of countries with stronger institutions, their slope coefficients would also increase, and the spread in the sensitivity of returns to oil prices between low- and high-institutional quality countries would be larger.

We should emphasize that our intention is not to accurately measure how institutional quality

---

[9]   Let D and E be the amount of debt and equity issued by a firm. Also, let β_1^E be the predictive slope calculated using stock returns. The predictive slope that is applicable to asset values can be calculated from leverage (D/E) and β_1^E as follows: $\beta_1^A = \frac{\beta_1^E}{1+D/E}$.

affects fiscal policy, but to gauge the approximate magnitude of its implications on the expenditure of oil revenue using a simple methodology that is applicable to panels of commodity-exporting countries. Below we discuss the main limitations of our analysis, which originate from data constraints.

In some countries, the market capitalization of listed companies is relatively low compared to GDP. The Canadian stock market, for instance, is about three times as large as its Indonesian counterpart (see Table 1). Such difference raises the question of whether the effect of oil price on equity returns, as measured for listed companies, can be generalized to non-listed companies, and whether the ability to generalize varies significantly across countries. Cross-country variation is especially important to us because our conclusions are based on comparing countries across the spectrum of institutional quality.

The first source of cross-country variation is that listed companies in a country may not be representative of the financing decisions of all firms – listed and non-listed – in that economy. The difference lies in leverage, since small companies in countries with more developed financial systems may have better access to debt than their counterparts in countries with less developed financial markets. A study of the differences in financing decisions between listed and non-listed firms across countries is an interesting question. Unfortunately, due to unavailability of data, it cannot be addressed in our study.

Second, there could be a compositional effect, because listed companies could be disproportionately more active in oil-related sectors in countries for which oil exports are more important. However, predictability does not appear to be related to the size of oil exports to GDP (Figure 3). For instance, Indonesia (which has the second-strongest predictability) has an oil export/GDP ratio similar to Canada (whose returns are the least predictable).

4. Conclusions

We study whether stock market returns in oil-exporting countries can be predicted by oil price changes, and we investigate the link between predictability and the quality of each country's institutions, which we measure with perceived corruption levels. Returns are predictable for about half the countries we consider, and predictability is stronger when institutional quality is lower.

We argue that the relation between predictability and institutional quality reflects the preference of countries with weaker institutions to consume oil windfalls locally through pro-cyclical fiscal policies, rather than smooth out the impact of windfalls by, for instance, investing the proceeds abroad. Within this framework, our results can be used to gauge the approximate magnitude of institutional quality's impact on how oil revenue is spent.

References

Alesina, A., G. Tabellini, and F. Campante, 2008, "Why is fiscal policy often procyclical?," *Journal of the European Economic Association*, 6(5), 1006–1036.

Amihud, Y., C. Hurvich, and Y. Wang, 2009, "Multiple–predictor regressions: hypothesis testing," *Review of Financial Studies*, 22(1), 413–434.

Barsky, R., and L. Kilian, 2004, "Oil and the macroeconomy since the 1970s," *Journal of Economic Perspectives*, 18(4), 115–134.

Campbell, J., and R. Shiller, 1988, "The dividend-price ratio and expectations of future dividends and discount factors," *Review of Financial Studies*, 1(3), 195–228.

Campbell, J., and S. Thompson, 2008, "Predicting excess stock returns our of sample: can anything beat the historical average?," *Review of Financial Studies*, 21(4), 1509–1531.

Driesprong, G., B. Jacobsen, and B. Maat, 2008, "Striking oil: another puzzle?," *Journal of Financial Economics*, 89(2), 307–327.

Ebeke, C., L. Omgba, and R. Laajaj, 2015, "Oil, governance and the (mis)allocation of talent in developing countries," *Journal of Development Economics*, 114, 126–141.

Esfahani, H., K. Mohaddes, and M. Pesaran, 2014, "An empirical growth model for major oil exporters," *Journal of Applied Econometrics*, 29(1), 1–21.

Fama, E., and K. French, 1988, "Dividend yields and expected stock returns," *Journal of Financial Economics*, 22(1), 3–25.

Fatás, A., and I. Mihov, 2003, "The case for restricting fiscal policy discretion," *Quarterly Journal of Economics*, 118(4), 1419–1447.

Fisman, R., and E. Miguel, 2007, "Corruption, norms, and legal enforcement: evidence from diplomatic parking tickets," *Journal of Political Economy*, 115(6), 1020–1048.

Goyal, A., and I. Welch, 2008, "A comprehensive look at the empirical performance of equity premium prediction," *Review of Financial Studies*, 21(4), 1455–1508.

Hamilton, J., 1983, "Oil and the macroeconomy since World War II," *Journal of Political Economy*, 91(2), 228–248.

———— , 1996, "This is what happened to the oil price-macroeconomy relationship," *Journal of Monetary Economics*, 38(2), 215–220.

———— , 2011, "Nonlinearities and the macroeconomic effects of oil prices," *Macroeconomic Dynamics*, 15(S3), 364–378.

Hong, H., W. Torous, and R. Valkanov, 2007, "Do industries lead stock markets?," *Journal of Financial Economics*, 83(2), 367–396.

Huang, R., R. Masulis, and H. Stoll, 1996, "Energy shocks and financial markets," *Journal of Futures Markets*, 16(1), 1–27.

Ichino, A., and G. Maggi, 2000, "Work environment and individual background: explaining regional shirking differentials in a large Italian firm," *Quarterly Journal of Economics*, 115(3), 1057–1090.

James, A., 2015, "The resource curse: a statistical mirage?," *Journal of Development Economics*, 114, 55–63.

Jones, C., and G. Kaul, 1996, "Oil and the stock markets," *Journal of Finance*, 51(2), 463–491.

Kaufmann, D., A. Kraay, and M. Mastruzzi, 2005, "Governance matters IV: governance indicators for 1996–2004," *Policy Research Working Paper no. 3630, World Bank, Washington, DC.*

———— , 2006, "Governance matters V: governance indicators for 1996–2005," *Policy Research Working Paper no. 4012, World Bank, Washington, DC.*

Kilian, L., 2008, "The economic effects of energy price shocks," *Journal of Economic Literature*, 46(4), 871–909.

Kilian, L., and C. Park, 2009, "The impact of oil price shocks on the U.S. stock market," *International Economic Review*, 50(4), 1267–1287.

Kotter, J., and U. Lel, 2011, "Friends or foes? Target selection decisions of sovereign wealth funds and their consequences," *Journal of Financial Economics*, 101(2), 360–381.

La Porta, R., F. Lopez-De-Silanes, A. Shleifer, and R. Vishny, 1997, "Legal determinants of external finance," *Journal of Finance*, 52(3), 1131–1150.

Leite, C., and J. Weidmann, 1999, "Does Moher Nature corrupt? Natural resources, corruption, and economic growth," *IMF Working Paper.*

Mauro, P., 1995, "Corruption and growth," *Quarterly Journal of Economics*, 110(3), 681–712.

Mehlum, H., K. Moene, and R. Torvik, 2006, "Institutions and the resource curse," *Economic Journal*, 116(508), 1–20.

Pastor, L., and R. Stambaugh, 2003, "Liquidity risk and expected stock returns," *Journal of Political Economy*, 111(3), 642–685.

Persson, T., 2002, "Do political institutions shape economic policy?," *Econometrica*, 70(3), 883–905.

Pieschacon, A., 2012, "The value of fiscal discipline for oil-exporting countries," *Journal of Monetary Economics*, 59(3), 250–268.

Ravazzolo, F., and P. Rothman, 2013, "Oil and U.S. GDP: a real-time out-of-sample examination," *Journal of Money, Credit and Banking*, 45(2-3), 449–463.

Sachs, J., and A. Werner, 1995, "Natural resource abundance and economic growth," *NBER Working Paper 5398.*

Stambaugh, R., 1999, "Predictive regressions," *Journal of Financial Economics*, 54(3), 375–421.

van der Ploeg, F., 2011, "Natural resources: curse or blessing?," *Journal of Economic Literature*, 49(2), 366–420.

Vicente, P., 2010, "Does oil corrupt? Evidence from a natural experiment in West Africa," *Journal of Development Economics*, 92(1), 28–38.

Figure 1

Institution quality and the size of sovereign wealth funds

The vertical axis shows the logarithm of the percentage ratio of total assets held in sovereign wealth funds for a given country over the GDP of the country. For Canada, the chart shows Alberta's Heritage Fund and Alberta's GDP.

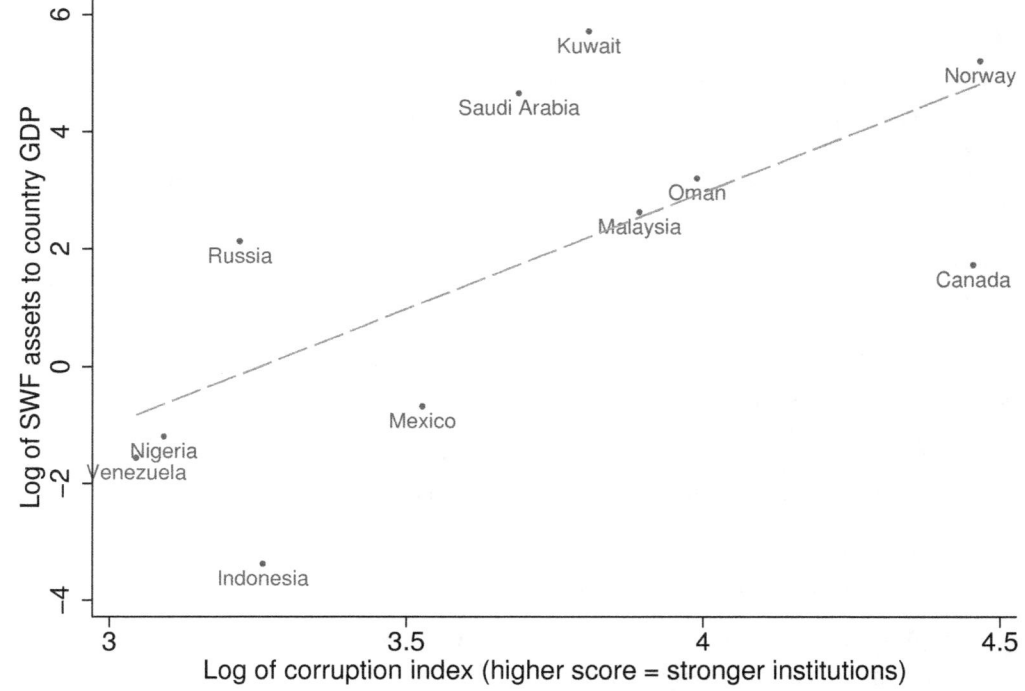

Figure 2

Corruption and stock return predictability

For each country, the charts plot the slopes of predictive regressions against the corresponding log-CPIs. Red markers show countries for which the slopes are statistically significant. Each chart indicates whether contemporaneous S&P 500 excess returns are included, and the number of days by which the oil time series is lagged.

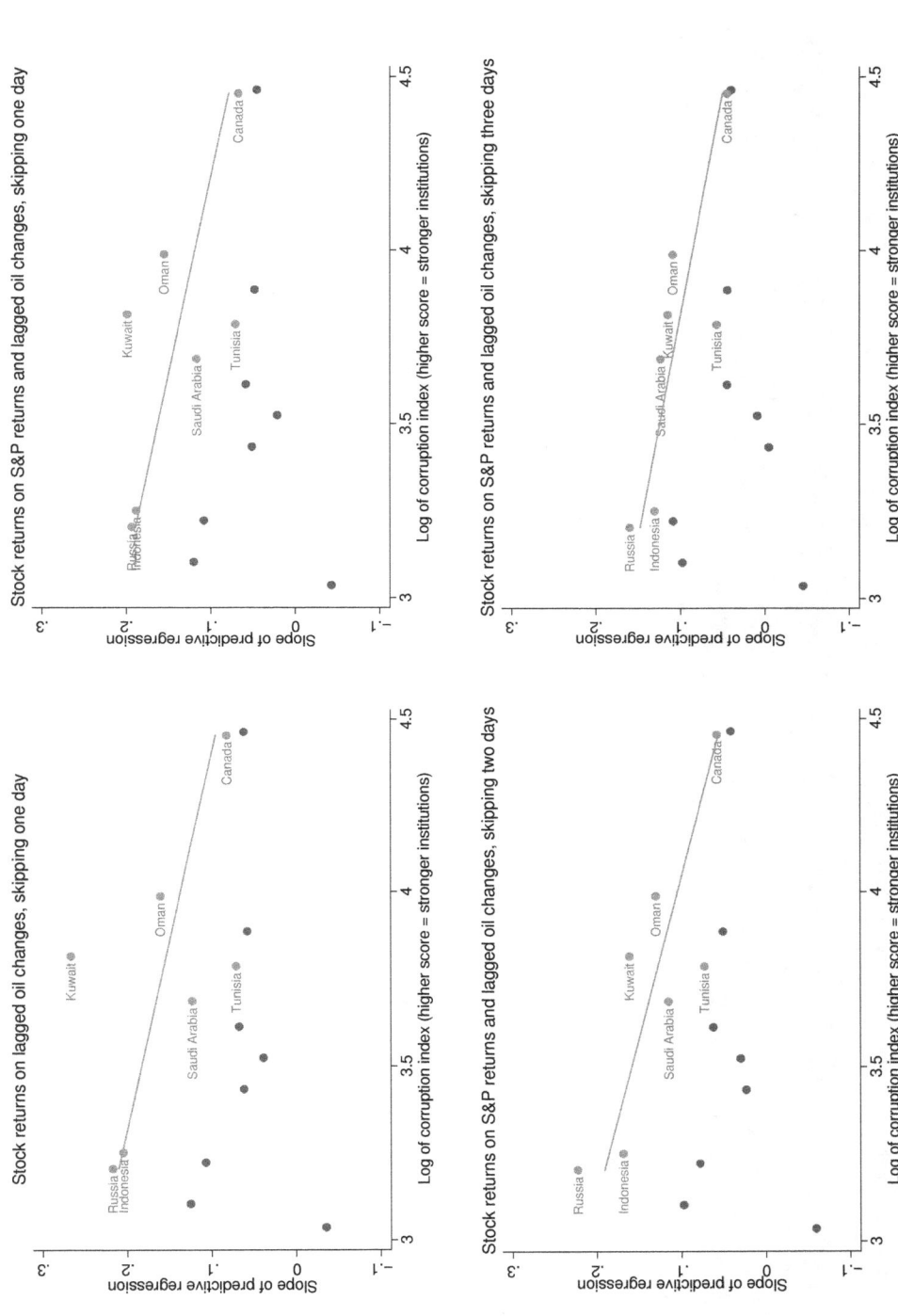

Figure 3

Corruption index and stock return predictability: possible alternative explanations

For each country, the charts plot the slopes of predictive regressions against the corresponding log-CPIs, private-sector domestic credit to GDP, capitalization of listed companies to GDP, and oil revenue to GDP. Red markers show countries for which the slopes are statistically significant. Regressions include contemporaneous S&P 500 excess returns and daily oil prices are lagged by two days.

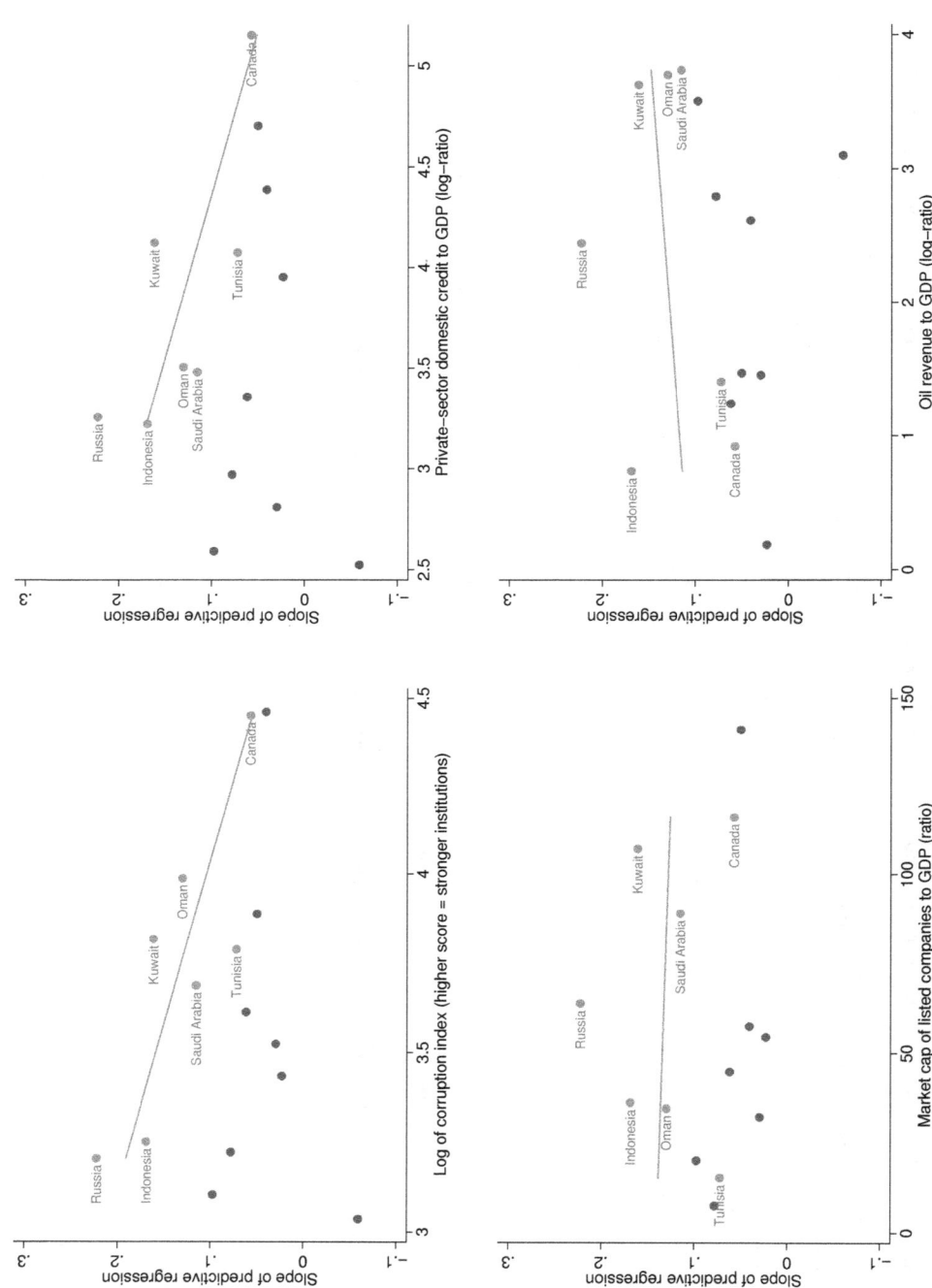

Figure 4

Corruption index and stock return predictability: additional robustness checks

For each country, the charts plot the slopes of predictive regressions against the corresponding log-CPIs when (1) excluding the October 2008 oil price change; (2) using Brent oil prices instead of WTI oil prices; (3) returns exclude dividends; (4) replacing contemporaneous S&P 500 returns with the S&P 500 lagged price-dividend yield as a regressor. Red markers show countries for which the slopes are statistically significant. Unless specified otherwise, regressions include contemporaneous S&P 500 excess returns and daily oil prices are lagged by two days.

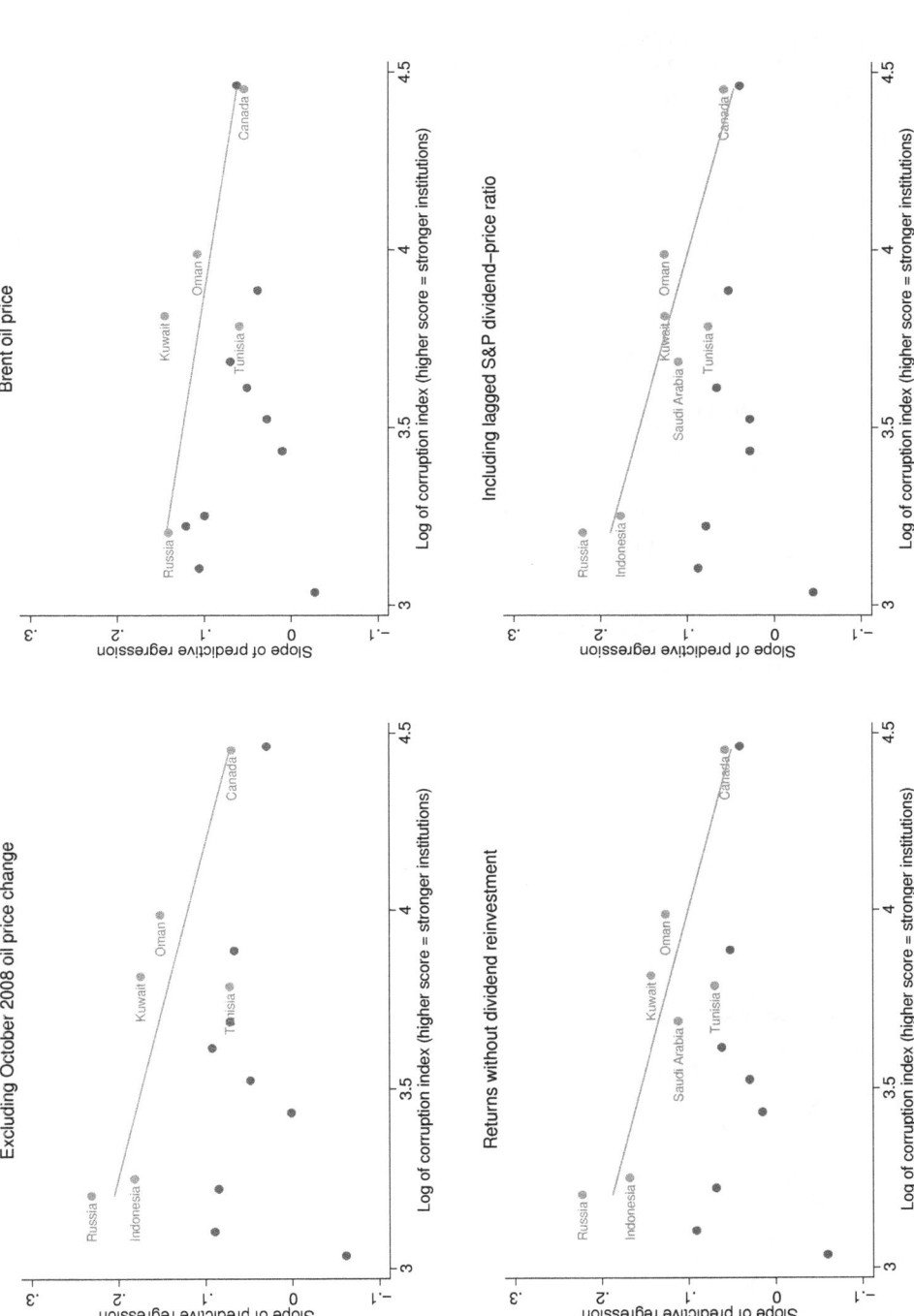

Table 1

Value of oil exports and of listed companies relative to gross domestic product (GDP)

The table shows the value of oil exports and of listed companies relative to GDP, in percent. Annual exports of crude oil (including lease condensate) are from the U.S. Energy Information Administration, and they are multiplied by the average annual WTI price. Current GDP in U.S. dollars is from the World Bank (series NY.GDP.MKTP.CD). The ratio of the market capitalization of listed companies to GDP is provided by the World Bank (series CM.MKT.LCAP.GD.ZS). Countries are sorted on the basis of the value of oil exports to GDP in 1995. Countries for which we are unable to source stock return data are shown in italics.

	Oil exports to GDP (%)			Stock market to GDP (%)		
Country	1995	2003	2010	1995	2003	2010
Nigeria	40	36	18	7	14	14
Oman	38	40	35	14	23	34
Saudi Arabia	30	36	38	29	73	67
Kuwait	29	30	34	53	124	100
Iran	*19*	*19*	*16*	*7*	*25*	*20*
Venezuela	16	21	12	5	5	1
Norway	11	14	11	30	42	60
Trinidad and Tobago	*7*	*9*	*11*	*21*	*94*	*59*
Ecuador	7	9	15	11	7	8
Egypt	4	1	1	13	33	38
Russia	4	12	9	4	54	66
Malaysia	3	4	3	251	153	166
Indonesia	3	3	1	33	23	51
Tunisia	3	2	5	22	9	24
Mexico	3	3	4	26	17	43
Colombia	2	3	5	19	15	73
Canada	1	2	3	61	101	134

Table 2

Summary statistics

The first column shows the average between 2003 and 2013 of the Corruption Perceptions Index (CPI). 2003 is the first year in which all the countries listed in the table are ranked by Transparency International. For the 15 countries we study, the remaining columns report summary statistics and other information for the monthly excess log-returns on stock indexes with reinvested dividends. The last three lines show statistics for monthly excess log-returns on the S&P 500 index, and monthly log-changes in the price of West Texas Intermediate (WTI) oil and Brent oil. Returns in percent. The sample ends in 2013.

	CPI	Return statistics				Details on return time series		
		Mean	Std. Dev.	Skewn.	Kurtosis	Starting date	Provider	Ticker
Nigeria	22	1.14	8.68	-0.49	8.89	1995/07	S&P	IFGDNG$
Oman	54	0.87	5.79	-1.35	10.90	2000/05	S&P	IFGDOM$
Saudi Arabia	40	0.79	7.39	-0.84	5.09	1998/01	S&P	IFGDSB$
Kuwait	45	0.37	6.99	-0.31	4.50	2005/01	S&P	IFGDKW$
Venezuela	21	0.96	13.50	-1.14	9.57	1995/01	Datastream	TOTMVE$
Norway	87	0.54	8.09	-1.33	7.98	1995/01	MSCI	MSNWAY$
Ecuador	25	0.00	9.83	-1.87	22.33	1996/01	S&P	IFFMEC$
Egypt	31	0.96	9.44	0.01	4.70	1995/01	MSCI	MSEGYT$
Russia	25	0.82	15.85	-1.08	8.80	1995/01	MSCI	MSRUSS$
Malaysia	49	0.17	8.40	-0.27	8.15	1995/01	MSCI	MSMALF$
Indonesia	26	0.15	13.32	-0.62	5.86	1995/01	MSCI	MSINDF$
Tunisia	44	0.02	5.06	-0.28	5.68	1996/01	S&P	IFFMTU$
Mexico	34	0.72	8.52	-1.30	6.95	1995/01	MSCI	MSMEXF$
Colombia	37	0.93	9.18	-0.44	4.11	1995/01	MSCI	MSCOLM$
Canada	86	0.66	6.14	-1.14	7.03	1995/01	MSCI	MSCNDA$
S&P 500		0.38	4.50	-0.88	4.54			
WTI		0.75	9.73	-0.64	4.35			
Brent		0.84	10.66	-0.64	4.91			

Table 3

The Corruption Perceptions Index over time

The table shows the Corruption Perceptions Index (CPI) in three years for each country. Note that the index was reported on a scale from 1 to 10 before 2012, and the values in 2003 and 2008 have been multiplied by 10.

	CPI		
Country	2003	2008	2013
Nigeria	14	27	25
Oman	63	55	47
Saudi Arabia	45	35	46
Kuwait	53	43	43
Venezuela	24	19	20
Norway	88	79	86
Ecuador	22	20	35
Egypt	33	28	32
Russia	27	21	28
Malaysia	52	51	50
Indonesia	19	26	32
Tunisia	49	44	41
Mexico	36	36	34
Colombia	37	38	36
Canada	87	87	81

Table 4

Predictive regressions, one month ahead

The table shows coefficients, t-stats, and adjusted R^2s from regressions of monthly excess stock returns on lagged changes in the price of WTI oil. The three rightmost columns of each panel show results from regressions of monthly excess stock returns on lagged changes in the price of WTI oil and contemporaneous excess returns on the S&P 500 index.

Panel A

Country		oil^a_{t-1}	oil^b_{t-1}	oil^c_{t-1}	With cont. S&P returns		
					oil^a_{t-1}	oil^b_{t-1}	oil^c_{t-1}
Canada	slope	0.0818	0.0763	0.0685	0.0672	0.0573	0.0447
	t-stat	1.74	1.84	1.81	2.35	2.05	1.73
	R^2_{adj}	0.012	0.010	0.009			
Colombia	slope	0.0675	0.0736	0.0593	0.0585	0.0619	0.0446
	t-stat	0.97	1.12	0.98	0.91	0.97	0.74
	R^2_{adj}	0.001	0.002	0.000			
Ecuador	slope	0.1070	0.0764	0.1060	0.1081	0.0781	0.1089
	t-stat	0.94	0.74	0.98	0.96	0.76	1.02
	R^2_{adj}	0.007	0.001	0.008			
Egypt	slope	0.0618	0.0370	0.0127	0.0512	0.0232	-0.0047
	t-stat	0.79	0.49	0.17	0.80	0.38	-0.08
	R^2_{adj}	0.000	-0.003	-0.004			
Indonesia	slope	0.2049	0.1903	0.1576	0.1884	0.1689	0.1308
	t-stat	1.97	1.93	1.76	2.10	1.94	1.66
	R^2_{adj}	0.018	0.015	0.010			
Kuwait	slope	0.2665	0.2221	0.1793	0.1989	0.1614	0.1150
	t-stat	3.26	3.07	2.75	2.68	2.38	1.82
	R^2_{adj}	0.123	0.091	0.066			
Malaysia	slope	0.0578	0.0630	0.0600	0.0481	0.0504	0.0441
	t-stat	0.90	0.99	1.02	0.81	0.84	0.79
	R^2_{adj}	0.000	0.001	0.001			
Mexico	slope	0.0388	0.0524	0.0375	0.0214	0.0297	0.0089
	t-stat	0.62	0.95	0.74	0.56	0.82	0.26
	R^2_{adj}	-0.002	-0.001	-0.002			

Panel B

Country		oil^a_{t-1}	oil^b_{t-1}	oil^c_{t-1}	With cont. S&P returns		
					oil^a_{t-1}	oil^b_{t-1}	oil^c_{t-1}
Nigeria	slope	0.1250	0.1041	0.1070	0.1200	0.0974	0.0979
	t-stat	1.35	1.20	1.39	1.42	1.22	1.37
	R^2_{adj}	0.016	0.010	0.012			
Norway	slope	0.0617	0.0623	0.0666	0.0453	0.0409	0.0397
	t-stat	0.97	1.07	1.21	0.98	0.95	1.02
	R^2_{adj}	0.001	0.001	0.003			
Oman	slope	0.1607	0.1354	0.1166	0.1553	0.1302	0.1092
	t-stat	2.84	2.85	2.95	3.16	2.96	2.77
	R^2_{adj}	0.071	0.05	0.041			
Russia	slope	0.2173	0.2533	0.1987	0.1937	0.2226	0.1601
	t-stat	1.94	2.45	2.01	2.09	2.50	1.87
	R^2_{adj}	0.014	0.020	0.012			
Saudi Arabia	slope	0.1229	0.1234	0.1320	0.1167	0.1153	0.1236
	t-stat	1.94	1.90	2.05	2.06	1.97	2.16
	R^2_{adj}	0.024	0.024	0.031			
Tunisia	slope	0.0711	0.0729	0.0576	0.0707	0.0724	0.0569
	t-stat	2.08	2.11	1.76	2.10	2.11	1.75
	R^2_{adj}	0.015	0.016	0.009			
Venezuela	slope	-0.0355	-0.0493	-0.0327	-0.0429	-0.0590	-0.0450
	t-stat	-0.48	-0.66	-0.50	-0.61	-0.83	-0.71
	R^2_{adj}	-0.004	-0.003	-0.004			

Table 5

Predictive regressions, including three lags of oil changes

The table shows coefficients and t-stats from regressions of monthly excess stock returns on up to three lags of changes in the price of WTI oil. The three rightmost columns show results from regressions of monthly excess stock returns on lagged changes in the price of WTI oil and contemporaneous excess returns on the S&P 500 index.

	Country	oil^a_{t-1}	oil^a_{t-2}	oil^a_{t-3}	With cont. S&P returns oil^a_{t-1}	oil^a_{t-2}	oil^a_{t-3}
slope	Canada	0.0779	0.0694	0.0451	0.0669	0.0093	-0.0084
t-stat		1.68	1.42	1.07	2.35	0.35	-0.32
slope	Indonesia	0.1990	0.1046	0.1140	0.1868	0.0379	0.0546
t-stat		1.92	1.01	1.24	2.06	0.40	0.71
slope	Kuwait	0.1820	0.1845	0.0802	0.1300	0.1436	0.0571
t-stat		2.71	2.61	1.06	2.13	1.90	0.98
slope	Oman	0.1560	0.0855	0.0912	0.1552	0.0545	0.0702
t-stat		2.93	2.11	2.18	3.14	1.41	1.70
slope	Russia	0.2118	0.1615	0.0957	0.1939	0.0639	0.0088
t-stat		1.93	1.79	0.92	2.08	0.78	0.09
slope	Saudi Arabia	0.1181	0.0559	0.0606	0.1121	0.0318	0.0284
t-stat		1.90	1.04	1.24	1.97	0.64	0.63
slope	Tunisia	0.0707	0.0208	-0.0011	0.0705	0.0192	-0.0025
t-stat		2.04	0.67	-0.03	2.06	0.62	-0.07